FOXES

ON THE

TRAMPOLINE

FOXES

ON THE

TRAMPOLINE

Charlotte Boulay

An Imprint of HarperCollinsPublishers

HarperCollins books may be purchased for educational, business, or sales promotional use. For information please e-mail the Special Markets Department at SPsales@harpercollins.com.

FIRST EDITION

Designed by Suet Yee Chong

Library of Congress Cataloging-in-Publication Data has been applied for.

ISBN 978-0-06-230249-6

14 15 16 17 18   OV/RRD   10 9 8 7 6 5 4 3 2 1

For my family

You've got enough. And if there's something I didn't say, you could make it up.

—Cy Twombly

CONTENTS

THREE

ONE

FRUITS OF MY LABOR

I was working. Every time I dove into the pool,
      or woke in the dark to hear a night bird
calling, or waited through the late afternoon heat

for the bell to ring for tea. Passing time was a job—
my white arms and legs leaden,

      my hair limp with rain. I wanted affirmation.
I wanted other things too, but especially that.

Across the world, idle tractors soak their jaws
      in oil. A jet plumbs the sun and a trailer

hauls pigs; one pink ear flaps between the slats. Once
I saw a musician play

Paganini on Paganini's own violin. He stood, counting,
counting silently,

and when the orchestra reached his part he flipped
the instrument into the air and caught it under his chin.

WATSON AND THE SHARK

It used to be a surprise—round the corner
of the museum and there it was, a shark lunging
at the boy, nearly catching his hair in its teeth,
and the boat hook poised to plunge. I was five,

never told that the boy lost his right leg
at the knee. Copley hides his severed foot
in the swirling water, and I always wondered
where the blood on the shark's teeth came from.

His small marbled eye fixed on me. Children
aren't told nursery rhymes anymore, especially the gory
ones: *here comes a candle to light you to bed,*
here comes a chopper to chop off your head. Copley loved

the solemn glance, the family gathered
in the drawing room, the arm outstretched
that may never reach but always rests suspended;
the boy naked, drowning. I touched it.

For an instant my finger rested
on the shark's cold gray skin.
Then my mother's swift tug back
and an afternoon of saying I was sorry,

but secretly, I was glad. It was clammy
and wet, muscles seething under the surface.
As much as I wanted that boy saved,
I wanted him eaten.

BLACK EXCURSION #13

after Louise Nevelson

By the end of our last days, the trees were
budding pink—branches like pokers,
          spitting sparks into heaviest anvil blue.
What spring let fall fell hard,

it struck me here, between knee and rib,
          O my acetabulum, little hip
          ball-and-socket joint! Lightning
in the blacksmith sky, the half-light-
ening of our half-lives. A sheen of ozone

slicked the leaves and the air
          burned, a bitter pendulum
of pain, a finial wave.

Can we contain ourselves
and everything else too? Each rounded
surface, each sliver-sharp point

pushes for space against its neighbor.
Our lungs are just one balloon after
          and after another. You can keep on going.
You can go on out.

MURMURATION

The most birds I've ever seen.
What lives

the longest? Superlatives
are only sometimes useful. A sea of open beaks
and wing. Flip the quick one, melt the meticulous.

It's a sort of trick that color,
that sun-in-a-cup, and the rush

has no signature. How can we measure
the velocity, the distance from one trestle to another—

leaving the ground is different. Banking

and rising all together, there's no barre
at which to stand; the sandbank shifts underwater
as the clouds move correspondingly above.

Watch the birds: the sky parts and remakes itself

almost cruelly while we wait
for the next instruction:

now dance   now droop   now rest.

BOYS OF MY YOUTH

Each week I pried stones from the frogs, ran hands over fetlocks.

Gold palomino, black Morgan, a huff and a cirrus
of steam. Winter mornings light

muscled its way through the whitewashed boards.

I spread sawdust and watered. Pulled mane hairs out by the roots;
Appaloosa, pinto, roan. Did you touch me then?

My skin may still remember the weight
of hands. Air lightened and swept.
I stacked buckets, each upturned curve a carapace of desire,

shadows of palm straining
the weightless bulk of clouds, the stalks of corn stripped
bare, the rustling

of unsteady faith as when still a girl I lay
in haystacks, taut as a bowstring,

dreaming of horses.

PLANTING DAFFODILS

The Friar tells her, *Drink this*
potion and for a time you will be
as dead.   What? she says.
  Are you kidding? Only the earth
knows that faith. But this love is of the earth,
so when she sleeps, it's in darkness,
        a round weight curled in a paper shroud.

This fall, digging little graves, I can hear
   winter approaching like the war
that already rages, not with drumbeats and shots
but silence, a great lack
of lucidity and grace.   Too soon,
        deaths have begun:

fruit clipped by frost, a bird limp
by the mailbox in the morning,
   the flaming leaves—don't be distracted;
we're blighting landscapes one by one.
        It's hard to believe
that everything resurrects itself in time,
   some things with more reliability than others.

So is a rooted bulb a record
of a promise kept through winter. A truth we only half
believe: each hoary, twinned sprout becomes,
in the moment before she sees him,
   Juliet, waking to a clasp of arms,
        yellow trumpets crying.

SHIPBREAKING

Ships too die, twisted sharp
in Bangladesh. On the cutting beaches
        men solder in the tidal pools,
breathe burnt metal, chemical stick.

Dissembling: flares in the sand
& heaps of bolts
thick around as your wrist. It's swiftly
        broken, skimmed
like a sharp thumb cut.

Now they melt down the I bars
        & oxen tow the hulks away.
Smells of raw fire, fish salt coats
scaffolding planks & pulleys

for the welders
who split the hull
                to take it down.
Sing, sea cathedrals—ships
who used to be whole,

        bridge me back. Hiss &
spark, tanker, what's in
your hold? Chittagong

tethered at the waterline.
        How to disappear: the ocean:
wet heat, salt spray. Who needs

a savior? It's better to be
pieced; it's better to be nothing.

MISTAKEN

The caught balloon I thought
        was a hawk. Wooden lemon,

silk flower, washing machine
that I dreamed was the sea.

The tree black with crows
        I saw as the last
dark fall leaves, dead-end

corridor, open window only
newly cleaned glass.   Skinny

        mirror, what Saint Andrew
did, French for Russian, sugar
for salt. Your voice

in the crowd, the highway exit,
a cricket for my phone.

The lyric that said keep
a piece of meat with you, the movie

that ended
differently, happier,
        the story I can repeat

of the eighth Pleiade,
stargone, lost.

THE REMINDER

My father and I driving
through the mountains, through
small towns perched above lakes.

Winters would sock them in with snow,
but today the patterned trees, the eel-like trees
casting across the road, the sky a sheet

of beaten metal, a mottled fish belly
of cirrus and sun, the summer day
a real Bonnard: *beau*.

On a bridge over the Raquette River we slow;
four cop cars brace the sides, and as we
cruise past, I gawk at the body

of a man splayed on the pavement,
his wet shadow dripping after
being held under to drown.

Then we're climbing the hill, behind
a logging truck, back through the ordinary
signs selling cold beer, groceries, guns,

I think of Marthe, steeping
in a blue bath, the fruit on the table,
the day grown still. Light moves over

the mountains. I drop a knife at dinner,
and look up, expecting to see his jacket
winged with water, shoes swollen like bulbs.

READING IN BED

about the doping of moths for collection.
A glowing sheet backlit

hung in the trees the humid darkness
a hundred wings

drawn to the light, a sugar-water beacon,
oh, & to sex.

The tiny screen cupped in one hand I flick
the lit pages

which draw their own small brown moth
to my eyeball's glint

& it tangles in my lashes. Dope, me,
crushing its fine

down on my cheek rather than
blinking it free.

SENZA

Jane says her grandfather
cage-raised foxes. She remembers

them tense, their shining eyes
watching her move around the yard.

All month the wind bosses
the flippant leaves.

At the grocery store, she watches
children in line for balloons.

A boy tests the pull of the string,
lets it tug his arm to the sky, realizes

everything that can run wants to.
She still dreams of rising

in darkness, slipping the pins
from the locks. When he lets go,

a colored blur soars easily above
the cars, the crowd, his animal cry:

It's running away. His open fist
the sharp relief of being without.

Want, world, want. The ice cream
is melting. It's time to go home.

AT NIGHT YOU'RE NOT LONELY

although the Morse tap of rain on the roof
is as indecipherable

as the staccato of a fly at the sill.

It's late, and the radio rustles no new news:
abandoned horses roam the barren plains.

Something slips into the darkness—

the smell of beeswax, the imagining of sun
or a palm stroking your back, still hours until dawn.

There's a hollowness even in turning the pillow

for the cool on your cheek, the migration a forced march
into another country.

AUBADE WITH PERICARDIUM
AND VISITOR

What a wreck the sky is this morning, slashed
through the middle
      and all bloody at the seams.

        When the new moon falls
on the first of the month
it seems unlucky, such absorbing

darkness it's hard to get out of bed.
      I open my mouth to test a thought
by voicing it without a boundary of truth,

      and the heart in its watery
pillow slip clenches to cushion

itself from harm. Early I slipped outside
      and there was a fish on a line
beside the coppery lake

and a snake waited,
his black body thick as a wrist.

      It was such an easy meal he swallowed
it whole, jaw hinged open wide while

his body molded around it;
          I mean the fins
bulged in his throat as it slid down.

Songs ought to be sung,
and when possible,

stories ought to be told

as they happened,
        not from the shortest distance, not
unattached, not asleep.

Today I rose in the wreck
        but I didn't know what to keep,

the memory or what it left behind:
        you, small chair; you, empty belly;

you, knock on the dark door.

T W O

Think of a blue that will sustain us.
—Amy Newman

LUMINARY

I dreamt a sailor. I dreamt

a sea so blue it stretched the corners
of my sight. Each day the boat, the wind,
the water. Each night the voice:

my little zephyr we are
whistling in the dark.

I followed it. I left my lover
behind. This is not an allegory,
it's an allegation.

Sing me a shanty, sing me
a lullaby. To forget you
I invented another.

PALLIKOODAM

When it rained, even our shoes
turned green. The fan whirred
except when the power was out,
then we read by candlelight under
the mosquito net, or didn't:
I feared it going up
around us, a fuzz of flame.
We lived with animals: small lizards
darting up the walls, lines of tiny,
imperious ants. Every night
we tried to trap the rat
in the rafters, baiting him with banana
until finally we awoke to a
snap. We had a small television
and we watched old sitcoms, new
pop videos, the twin towers falling
again and again. They said over
and over that nothing would be
the same after that, and for once
they were right. We ate chocolate bars
for their sweet familiarity, and we lined
books neatly on the shelves. We slept
holding each other and woke in the mornings
to hear someone singing, softly,
as she swept the yard clean.

CALENTURE

A disease incident to sailors in the tropics, characterized by delirium in which the patient, it is said, fancies the sea to be green fields, and desires to leap into it. —OXFORD ENGLISH DICTIONARY

The way I get dizzy when I give blood,
red spheres slugging through the tube,

    or on TV when the president outlines
three points, each conflicting with the others, then

desert blowing everywhere,
    no green, not a blade in sight.

Come back, you said, but to me your lips read *jump.*

    Water as clear as the moment before waking
from a dream, then milky submission: I had my choice.

The way ginkgo trees wait until every leaf has turned
golden, then let them fall, all at once.

FEVER

Singing floats up from
the Rubber Board Road where the trees
       all lean to the left as if listening
       for a whisper
               didn't die the dark

Beyond the whine of a motor
       the swish of brooms
I am a drum beaten on both sides
even my freckles are hot
my hair like melted brass

didn't   *the dark*

Sweat winches its way down my side
rubber draining white from the vein
       congealed and ready to be scraped

Heat humming behind my eyes
the bones of my face mirrored through the skin

didn't die the dark

O for the trees limber and lost
frangipani white blooming

Give me the sea in a glass—I'll drink it down

FIELD

Light rises from the water in sheets,
a square luminescence repeating the outlines

of mirror, bedstead, door. If you move you must
steady yourself against the frame. Even the current
pressed against the slats of the hull

has become desirous: tongue and groove.

LOVE IS TO WATER AS FALLING IS TO

Last night I dreamt in Chinese, unfaithful
even to language.
            The air was sinking
in heat; through the window sailed
a luna moth, pale green wings

like dinner plates, antennae twitching.
It lit on my shoulder and then
        you knew how it was.

I've finished the analogy:

The space between migrating birds is to
distance as kneecap is to half-moon.

Water has its own language. I know the names
        of several bones in Spanish.
I know how to say good morning in Greek.

I know that the flocked birds are leaving
for India and that the moon pulls both our bodies
and the tide. So many things to know, and this
heat won't quit.

When I betrayed you it was night.
One leg already over the railing. My eyes closed

when I left when I lied when I jumped.

CATCHING THE PRAYING MANTIS

She's on the wall next to the photographs
      I hung of family. One captures
the sailor lying in the shallows, letting the water

lick his collarbones. Whoever took that picture
was standing in the water.
      There is no shoreline, only the dunes. No safe
place to stand.

She's emerald, big as a mango,
glistening and toothed.   Nights like this
they all come in, they can feel
      the pressure of monsoon
keening, a cello's deepest note.

Did you know I could take a photograph
of my sailor?   Well, not really, but there's a blur
      in the water that could be him. It always
could be him, if I look hard enough.

Move the cup over—no, the other way.
Slide your hand underneath. You've got her
imprisoned now, quick,
      the door's already open.
The night is black, clouds low.

She takes off out of your cupped palm with a sound
like a gentle clapping. The window's open:
ten minutes later she flies back in.

AUBADE WITH WHISTLE

Meen wallah meen wallah what do you fish

Birds scritching in the eaves
chuckling low

Every time I dove into the deep pool or woke hard

Slipping my own sunrise with a cry
burnt-metal rice
smoke clouding the room

I've come back to sing you to grant you a wish

The sea is a dream of heat and salt
and morning enters without a by-your-leave

I'll take it now to stop the kettle
the greensounds

the train driving through my sleep

LET ME WALK YOU HOME

The sky is an oyster, it spits
out a string of pearls, smooth as vanilla,
each gleam a cicada answering back.

     Oh, baby, my sweet treat baby
wails from a passing car. The sharp needles
of memory prick my heels. Shadows

light the street and buds close up,
     retracting their flowers.
What are you waiting for?
          What strange birds
will come mudskipping through this dark sky?
The sun will go out, leaving
everything the color of x-ray.

I want to be emptied
and to clasp your hands through water.
Je suis grise et perdue, arrêtes, arrêtes: now home

     to unlock the whistling gate and watch
as stars slip from the sky's maw,
little shining eyes on a string.

FALSE HELLEBORE

You wake, hair static around your head. It crackles
       in the friction of your hands.
Since we've returned

it's not the same. We're surrounded
by greenery: tangled vines and stands of clacking
       bamboo. Cluster of green bananas with a purple flower.
Burning rubber scents the salt air. I see
a plant imprinted

on the backs of my eyelids, impetuous, officious, a stripe
       down the middle of each leaf like a skunk's back—
it's trying to look
like something else. My hands press

the sheets smooth. I wish
       I didn't have to be over or under all the time,
just whelmed, not false and not true.

MIGRATION

Tonight a highway of birds in the sky
above the house, rasping south.

Not terns or kestrels, not kingfishers diving
from their rocky nests. These are inland fliers,

weathered and ready to follow each other
for as long as it takes. I woke with a fever,

and your hand on my neck was the rush of cool air
while bicycling down a rise. I listened,

but I couldn't hear when you mouthed the words.
There's a map of the bottom of the ocean

and I think I can speak to you there. The fever broke,
but remains in my muscles' memory. I see it

when I close my eyes: it looks like the shadow
of a ship. In sleep animals pass through my dreams.

I can name them—birds and horses carry me
through air, desire splintering, landing nowhere

FIELD

In these months you've become
invisible as a page turner.

Palm the rudder, imagine
                      turning it back. Currents startle
and mix, the sunset bloodied—   Enough.

The shadow of the boat tracks itself like a hunter.

IN HOSPITAL

Please lift your shirt
she said. She pulled at it
and laid her cool palm on

the rough white skin
of my back. I was surrounded
by fluorescent light and the room

was crowded with
women. The doctor looked at me and,
as though speaking to a stone,

gripped the long oiled black
braid at her neck, and the women
murmured in waves.

The heat of Kalathipady Junction
at dusk spread in a low purple sheet
and the night birds sang in a lapping chorus

heal. A drum beat evening prayers
in a dim-lit living room and I walked
toward it: alone.

DEAR SAILOR,

like stars through the sextant, your path
is fixed by curvature. At evening

cirrus stretches through the sky
and jellyfish cling to the rudder;

a castaway will phosphoresce. Weeks will turn
into months. Here they drew dragons.

We're past the edge of that map.
Shade your eyes against the moon's

bright hook; the calm glass flickers—
figures move underwater. *Is it a trick*

of the light? Rejoice. In the beginning
was nothing. In the beginning was green.

Orpheus, we have learned your lesson.
Our feet left the deck cleanly, eyes on what's below.

THREE

CHANGELING

We protect what we can. Often this means hiding things:
       good silver, heirlooms, send the children away.
              Say it's diphtheria or the war, they'll have better adventures

without parents anyway, as books show.
       Before the bombing they buried the stained glass
              of the cathedrals in France, easing the homilies

from their frames, swaddling the cobalt and crimson in quilts
       to keep them underground, safe.
              Still, the invaders arrive. And do those

who were hidden return? When I am sent,
       instead of being buried, I ascend to a strange
              blue country, sky folded cleanly as laundry.

I live in a house by the sea. At low tide I scratch the mud
       for snails, stones, bits of bottle frosted to jewels.
              When I wake each night, something is different.

I hear the echo of footsteps. The moon hungrily eyes
       a bowl of pears. Branches crack in the wind, syncopated
              with the wailing of furious cats. Next morning as I rearrange

what's been disturbed, each tumbled object I replace
       bears the mark of an unknown visitor.
              Should I have shut the windows at night? Illumined

the unwary house against every transformation?
      For years the cathedrals' flanks stood gaping,
            the translucent saints replaced by darkness.

Imagine morning in a field outside the city, a company of people,
      a growing murmur. The first cut into the scarred
            and salted loam, the clink of shovel on glass.

WHAT TO KEEP

At Lucerne, the bells rang
all day to celebrate—what?

We all had theories, but no one
       was sure. Parrots flickered

through the topiary calling *Henry—Henry—*
but he never came. We wondered
everywhere: on the path,

in the hot gold fields, clutching
the rails of the rattling truck bed.

We jumped bridges, chased dogs
down their own twisted drives.
       By day we passed farmers,

the Amish, the stragglers: berry season
ended, two more men out of work.
       Each morning we swam the lake, water
steaming around us.

Lucerne the summer house,
whitewashed skim as milk, garden

white too, pale carrots, wax apples; inside
       closets of things we had loved,

but always something missing, the lack
a wrenched clasp, a vaccination ache.

To keep it we would travel
        by night, slip between the pine trees
and the sea. The parrots rustled, the bells

relentless. The next time we visit,
who moves the path closer to the water?

Who leaves their breath hanging, unclaimed?

Then I enter a room where a nurse

pulls a rubber sheet over the table and a long bag. *I'm not
superstitious, I just have a feeling.*

I'm a little short; they fetch me a stool. The man

is blue around the lips. There's a flock of gloved hands.
Harder. *Harder.*   *Lock your elbows. Don't be afraid*

to break a rib.
I thought I'd feel sadder. I thought the still body

in its nakedness might seem unutterably sad. Someone

rises, and in another

crowded city someone sinks.
Fluorescence congeals

around our heads,

our hands rest in sticky pools
of light. I'm standing in my own kitchen

thinking of nothing.   A car squeals
on a turn, it's silent, then the click

of the spoons in their drawer.

MAP: LATE BLACKBERRIES

To start, head west. You'll pass an intersection
with a dry cleaner and a bankrupt
tavern on the corner, a fork to the right—

don't turn there. Once
you cross the old train tracks
turn left, past the hotel.

There's a pile of discarded
mattresses and a rusted-out Chevy.
The road twists and curves;

each corner of light meets
and turns away from the next:
a box, a box, a wave. Then you'll

see it. It's beautiful this time of year,
swampy and orange, the bent maples
trailing their leaves in the water,

and one heron alert as a traffic signal.
Some birds we used to sing to:
cormorant, cormorant, fly away

home, as you'll come, afterward, arms
laden with blue salvia and bittersweet,
hands stained and scratched. You should

go soon, the weather might change. All morning
I've watched squirrels corkscrew up tree trunks,
tiny squirrel hearts thumping in their chests.

WOLF TIDE

Have you run out of thunderbolts?

—THE TROJAN WOMEN

The curtain's a garden, flowers
faded on the reverse, meant to be admired
from the other side, twining round the rings,

their twin views reflected in double
mirrors: this could go on ad infinitum,
a mean gulp of savage undertow—

I'll eat you up I love you so—unless
I get between the two uncertain surfaces
and make it stop.

So I rise from the bath,
dripping on Euripides, toweling
dry the V of my thighs, my whole body

flushed from the water, pink as a ham,
my flat belly lovely and sad.
Does this tub have tides, the way the

moon pulls at my womb? I'm waiting
for the turn, stranded on sand;
I'm sloshing around: ebb, neap.

MARRIAGE

The lock on the door
is more than one hundred years old
and it almost got stuck the other day.

Someone used to bake bread in the oven
and lined shelves with gleaming preserves
and sweat every summer putting up

tomatoes, corn relish
and beans. You can see the ghosts
of footsteps in the cement

in the cellar, the depressions holding themselves
steady and each spring filling with water
as it seeps up through the clay.

Someone fitted the tongue-and-groove
porch ceiling, then lay on his back
afterward with a cold bottle, admiring

his work. On the phone, my mother
says it's time to get a new mattress.
She can see the outlines of my father's body,

and hers, lying next to each other
every time she changes the sheets.

TALKING TO THE DEAD

I'm thinking about "va-va-voom"—
       Is it an idea or an expression of the body,
of the rising pulse? You know when you see it,
       the opposite of the Delaware River in a March

without snow, its close-shaven banks
       pale gold and rumpled, all the warmth
beaten out. The towpath is barely gelid,
       edged with ice, and the water glowers

and the sky glowers back. Preparing for class
       I read in the *Norton*, "Hardy was dejected all his life,
even as a child . . ." Ridiculous, officious
       in the warm library, but here the trees are bare

as a whistle, and everything's brown
       and gray and the luminous, horrible gold
of that winter straw, like trickster straw
       that could be falsely spun, as if spring's riches

are contingent on good behavior, or the magical change
       of my own bad mood. Behind the train tracks
vines devour power lines, and a red glove,
       abandoned and luscious in the muddy grass,

is almost cheerfully sexual; it's trying too hard.
       All his life—now I'll have to explain
why that can't or can be written down on the exam.
       I taught *Tess* in India, once. Would that make up

for any of it? To know that she traveled to the banks
       of the Meenachil, to a classroom of hot brick
and earnest readers, straining to understand your sadness
       even as around us the monsoon va-va-voomed?

Afterward we undressed him. We saved
everything material, all the coins
in his pockets, his glasses, his cut-up pants.

Then the nurse covered him with a sheet,
a blanket. She crossed his blue-fingered
arms. Last, she combed his thinning

white hair, so it lay neatly on his brow.

I cannot picture her face, or remember
what she said as we smoothed
the blanket over his chest.

But I know that all of this was done briskly,
and all of it seemed as if it were
entirely the right and natural
thing to do.

ORACULAR

The road is too hot to move. I'm stuck in the median,
I slept too fast & then too slow.

Sufi says, *I'm not only bones & bones—*

who loves the saints in the streets? We don't need

your love, only your briefest notice sustains us.
Dogs crouch in the ancient of their shade,

tooth-brushers spit into their crevices, piss in the gutters
they create.
Bedtime—stars like mustard seeds pop

through the smog. There's a wail & an anguish of horns;

everlastingness reaches up & turns out the light—

THE END OF SUMMER

Waking facedown in the grass, her
crooked arm is asleep from the elbow up,
the numb shoulder as if it's already

gone, amputated in the dream
she was having of first frost, or

in that space in the mind left vacant
for images from the news. The tracings
        of stalks on her cheek

bisect each other, profile
    marked with the season
and across the water the outlines
of faraway houses could be any town.

        The calling insects can feel
the approaching silence and strain to break it;
her shoulder as it lifts pops softly, echoing

everything that came before: the IED, the line drive,
the cherry pit, the blundering june bug.

HONEY

For a tour of the town, go to my father,
who once told me that the feeling of weightlessness

just before sleep is a cellular memory of floating
in the ocean. The river floods the bridge in spring,

but we're proud of it, and of the new school, too small already.
The green around the empty church is heat-soaked, blind.

In the boat	*my back was aching*	*but I rowed across*
the river.	*My head was heavy,*	*Lord, but I kept*
thinking	*that on the other side*	*I'd be changed.*

In the crypt by the library they used
to pack the bodies in honey to keep them

through winter until faraway relatives arrived
for the funeral, then they placed the bodies

in the ground. If bees love
it is a golden color, sweet and plentiful and airless.

FLEET

1.

I labeled the folder "maybe-baby" and I kept it
hidden and counted days. I watched for signs:

the candle's fierce semaphore
flickering, the tulips bowing out of the vase,

the hot golden globe of my earring; the hiss of the stove.
I kissed the cat and the pillow, and the mouthpiece

of the phone. I kissed the wind as it passed my lips.
I dreamed satsumas, rose hips, sunrise, but now

the baby is dreaming the boats, and
the boats are burning.

2.

Sometimes on canvas a painter layers
one image over another—what's the term for that?

Or for what perspective reveals? My happiness was
mismatched and empty; an oar slid from the rowlock

like a ready tooth from the gum. The memory is colored
by my own retelling of routine: I tidied the garden,

snipped and weeded. I broke a small, unfinished
bisque-ware bowl and was glad. I covered the loss

in the trash beneath strata of coffee grounds
and peelings—the underpainting, the wash.

3.

The baby swam in fox fire, its limbs weightless
and prickling with light. On the bowsprit watch

I always sang out last, missing the passing ships
and obstacles because I was distracted by the collision

of current and cloud, and by other multitudinous griefs.
Remember: the garden, the fireworks, the glowing

bulbs; the clots like jellied poppies, the ecstatic
backache, the firefly rush to the head. Shove an oar

toward the histories, the hoards, the retreat into
ash, the missing, the cries, the horrible fluorescent birth.

4.

After the bloom of battle faded,
the oarsmen foundered in the smoke.

They hallooed till they were hoarse, then
they hosannaed, they wept. They finally fetched up

a flotilla of boats and stumbled, soaked, together.
And as they tallied themselves, talking

softly and counting the living and the dead,
the sky blazed inexorable; a cold wash of waves

ate at their ankles, and by the entrails they divined
that this was not God, but something wilder.

5.

Some battle, still burning today, some
common occurrence, more normal

than not, no cause for alarm. I'm learning to arm
against the fog of hope, to plug leaks

in the body's boat with moss and tape. Listen:
underwater after four nights of rain

a voice is singing *haul away, back again.* Perhaps
the child was saved by an army, tattered and sore,

chained in the galleys, afeared of fire, rowing
rowing their boats to shore.

6.

All autumn I watched women grow round as ticks.
Later I gazed into the darkening glass

or stood blank in grocery aisles. Want is the old fairy tale:
trying to carry the sea in a sieve.

Losing too is still ours; forgetting is the crescent moon—
its shadowed bulk strains.

The traitor tide turns and floats
the lost ones to the surface. Remember?

Release: when we sleep, we wait inside the circle.
It draws around us its unbroken, marvelous curve.

THE DISTANT

In the morning everything was rustling:
the moon as it fell behind the trees,

a thousand creatures in the hedge. Noise when
I opened the door:

appeal, appeal, said a bird, but
I did not answer. Even the thistles

had halos as the field
shimmered to a point

where motes of pollen
thickened the air and parted as I
moved through it. Reticules,

minarets of cattails
and birds waking mid-flight,

and in that imperfect darkness
of the visible frame, a stranger's presence of mind

turned away from grief.
I let it go:
hard eye: bright thought: down stream.

FOXES ON THE TRAMPOLINE

Mostly, I want to look out the window
before anyone has risen
and see them,
   slim red bodies at first hesitant,
then long spines twisting with delight—

to find the ground so suddenly springy!
One jumps and the other bounces
and their silky fur flies.
   They look too skinny, they need

to steal a chicken, or perhaps I could
put out some milk and bread—no. What is this,
some kind of story?

Sometimes you ask, do you want something
that is not available to you right now? Next door
   a man coughs and coughs.
A tremor runs through me.

I would never tell them I am watching them
pretend to fly; trespassers, all of us,
of this easy, weightless secret.

   What I want is folded up somewhere,
or buried, or slipped under the sea. I have everything
else, everything everything. O fox,
is this joy?

AMERICAN SONGBOOK

Who wants to keep their animal selves close?

That blackbird at my window—I sent it away.

      We speed toward long shorelines and most
can't see where we'll end up: it's hard to say.

Make my bed, light the light, lean over and listen:

I was mistaken and woke to the train passing through,
      call foggy with sorrow as a glass of milk.

I fastened its voice
to every memory of you. Goodnight, Irene,

in the land of dreamy-dreams, we're eating miles now,

driving into the night. Not lost and gone forever; I'm staying,
it seems, waiting
         for the chance to sing it right: This world

is trouble through which I'm treading my way.

I've been working on the rail
road, all the   livelong   day.

The poem "Watson and the Shark" refers to the painting of the same name by John Singleton Copley.

"The Reminder" is indebted to Nancy Willard.

"At Night You're Not Lonely" is or was the name of a Chinese call-in radio show popular with young migrant workers. Peter Hessler describes the show in his book *Oracle Bones*.

The word *pallikoodam* means "school" in Malayalam, the language of Kerala, India.

"False Hellebore" is also the title of a photograph by Imogen Cunningham.

"Oracular" refers to the many tombs that still exist in the streets of Delhi.

"Fleet" was partially inspired by Cy Twombly's series *Lepanto*. Lepanto was a naval battle between the Ottoman Turks and the "Holy League" of Spain, Venice, and the Papacy in 1571. Wikipedia notes that "Lepanto was the last major naval battle fought almost entirely between oar-powered galleys." The last section of "Fleet" contains lines from Rilke's "For Hans Carossa."

It is possible to watch short home videos of foxes jumping on trampolines on YouTube.

acknowledgments

Thanks to the editors of the following publications, where these poems appeared, sometimes in slightly different forms:

"Fruits of My Labor" and "American Songbook" in *Crazyhorse*
"Watson and the Shark," "Calenture," "Let Me Walk You Home," and
    "False Hellebore" in *Boston Review*
"Oracular" and "Murmuration" in *The Adroit Journal*
"Boys of My Youth" and "Aubade with Pericardium and Visitor" in
    Michigan Quarterly Review
"Planting Daffodils" in *Slate*
"Shipbreaking" in *Field*
"Mistaken" in *The Massachusetts Review*
"Changeling" in *Cyphers*
"Talking to the Dead" in *The New Yorker*
"Honey" and "Fleet" in *The Pinch*

Thank you, tireless teachers, readers, friends: Britta Ameel, Natalie Bakopoulos, Dargie Anderson Bowersock, Kathy Calkins, Jeremiah Chamberlin, George Cooper, John Whittier Ferguson, Linda Gregerson, Lorna Goodison, Suzanne Hancock, Lizzie Hutton, Thomas Lynch, Khaled Mattawa, Raymond McDaniel, Patrick O'Keeffe, Mary Roy, Preeta Samarasan, Natalia Singer, Ann Sjostedt, the St. Andrew's Writers Group, Elizabeth Ames Staudt, Richard Tillinghast, Cyrill Wolf. Thank you, Albert Glover, for your immense generosity. Thank you, Dan Halpern. Thank you, Harvey, Shirley, Roger, and Phillip Dekker Boulay, and thank you, Family Girard. Finally, first and last, thanks and love, Brian Girard, for everything.

"Fruits of My Labor" is for Dargie.

"Foxes on the Trampoline" is for Ann.